Sex in Mind and in Education

Henry Maudsley

educational strain will commence about the time
when, by the development of the sexual system, a
great revolution takes place in the body and mind,
and an extraordinary expenditure of vital energy is
made, and will continue through those years after
puberty when, by the establishment of periodical
functions, a regularly recurring demand is made
upon the resources of a constitution that is going
through the final stages of its growth and development. The energy of a human body being a definite and not inexhaustible quantity, can it bear,
without injury, an excessive mental drain as well as
the natural physical drain which is so great at that
time? Or, will the profit of the one be to the detriment of the other? It is a familiar experience
that a day of hard physical work renders a man in-
capable of hard mental work, his available energy
having been exhausted. Nor does it matter greatly
by what channel the energy be expended; if it be
used in one way it is not available for use in another. When Nature spends in one direction, she must
economize in another direction. That the development of puberty does draw heavily upon the vital
resources of the female constitution, needs not to
be pointed out to those who know the nature of the
important physiological changes which then take
place. In persons of delicate constitution who have
inherited a tendency to disease, and who have little
vitality to spare, the disease is apt to break out at
that time; the new drain established having de-
prived the constitution of the vital energy neces-

2

sary to withstand the enemy that was lurking in it.
The time of puberty and the years following it are
therefore justly acknowledged to be a critical time
for the female organization.   The real meaning of
the physiological changes which constitute puberty
is, that the woman is thereby fitted to conceive and
bear children, and undergoes the bodily and mental
changes that are connected with the development
of the reproductive system.   At each recurring period there are all the preparations for conception,
and nothing is more necessary to the preservation
of female health than that these changes should take
place regularly and completely.   It is true that
many of them are destined to be fruitless so far as
their essential purpose is concerned, but it would
be a great mistake to suppose that on that account
they might be omitted or accomplished incomplete-
ly, without harm to the general health.   They are
the expressions of the full physiological activity of
the organism.   Hence it is that the outbreak of disease is so often heralded, or accompanied, or fol-
lowed by suppression or irregularity of these functions.   In all cases they make a great demand upon
the physiological energy of the body : they are sensitive to its sufferings, however these be caused ;
and, when disordered, they aggravate the mischief
that is going on.

When we thus look the matter honestly in the
face, it would seem plain that women are marked
out by nature for very different offices in life from
those of men, and that the healthy performance of

her special functions renders it improbable she will succeed, and unwise for her to persevere, in running over the same course at the same pace with him. For such a race she is certainly weighted unfairly. Nor is it a sufficient reply to this argument to allege, as is sometimes done, that there are many women who have not the opportunity of getting married, or who do not aspire to bear children ; for whether they care to be mothers or not, they cannot dispense with those physiological functions of their nature that have reference to that aim, however much they might wish it, and they cannot disregard them in the labor of life without injury to their health. They cannot choose but to be women : cannot rebel successfully against the tyranny of their organization, the complete development and function whereof must take place after its kind. This is not the expression of prejudice nor of false sentiment ; it is the plain statement of a physiological fact. Surely, then, it is unwise to pass it by ; first or last it must have its due weight in the determination of the problem of woman's education and mission ; it is best to recognize it plainly, however we may conclude finally to deal with it.

It is sometimes said, however, that sexual difference ought not to have any place in the culture of the mind, and one hears it affirmed with an air of triumphant satisfaction that there is no sex in mental culture. This is a rash statement, which argues want of thought or insincerity of thought in those who make it. There is sex in mind as distinctly as

there is sex in body ; and, if the mind is to receive
the best culture of which its nature is capable,
regard must be had to the mental qualities which
correlate differences of sex. To aim, by means of
education and pursuits in life, to assimilate the
female to the male mind, might well be pronounced
as unwise and fruitless a labor as it would be to
strive to assimilate the female to the male body by
means of the same kind of physical training and by
the adoption of the same pursuits. Without doubt
there have been some striking instances of extraordinary women who have shown great mental power,
and these may fairly be quoted as evidence in support of the right of women to the best mental
culture ; but it is another matter when they are
adduced in support of the assertion that there is no
sex in mind, and that a system of female education
should be laid down on the same lines, follow the
same method, and have the same ends in view, as a
system of education for men.

Let me pause here to reflect briefly upon the
influence of sex upon mind. In its physiological
sense, with which we are concerned here, mind is
the sum of those functions of the brain which are
commonly known as thought, feeling, and will.
Now, the brain is one among a number of organs
in the commonwealth of the body ; with these organs
it is in the closest physiological sympathy by definite paths of nervous communication, has special
correspondence with them by internuncial nerve-
fibers ; so that its functions habitually feel and

declare the influence of the different organs. There
is an intimate consensus of functions. Though it
is the highest organ of the body, the coördinating
center to which impressions go and from which
responses are sent, the nature and functions of the
inferior organs with which it lives in unity affect
essentially its nature as the organ of mental functions. It is not merely that disorder of a particular organ hinders or oppresses these functions, but
it affects them in a particular way; and we have
good reason to believe that this special pathological effect is a consequence of the specific physiological effect which each organ exerts naturally
upon the constitution and function of mind. A
disordered liver gives rise to gloomy feelings; a
diseased heart, to feelings of fear and apprehension;
morbid irritation of the reproductive organs, to
feelings of a still more special kind—these are
familiar facts; but what we have to realize is, that
each particular organ has, when not disordered, its
specific and essential influence in the production of
certain passions or feelings. From of old the influence has been recognized, as we see in the doctrine
by which the different passions were located in particular organs of the body; the heart, for example,
being made the seat of courage, the liver the seat
of jealousy, the bowels the seat of compassion; and
although we do not now hold that a passion is
aroused anywhere else than in the brain, we believe
nevertheless that the organs are represented in the
primitive passions, and that, when the passion is

aroused into violent action by some outward cause, it will discharge itself upon the organ and throw its functions into commotion. In fact, as the uniformity of thought among men is due to the uniform operation of the external senses, as they think alike because they have the same number and kind of senses, so the uniformity of their fundamental passions is due probably to the uniform operation of the internal organs of the body upon the brain; they feel alike because they have the same number and kind of internal organs. If this be so, these organs come to be essential constituents of our mental life.

The most striking illustration of the kind of organic action which I am endeavoring to indicate, is yielded by the influence of the reproductive organs upon the mind; a complete mental revolution being made when they come into activity. As great a change takes place in the feelings and ideas, the desires and will, as it is possible to imagine, and takes place in virtue of the development of their functions. Let it be noted, then, that this great and important mental change is different in the two sexes, and reflects the difference of their respective organs and functions. Before experience has opened their eyes, the dreams of a young man and maiden differ. If we give attention to the physiology of the matter, we see that it cannot be otherwise, and if we look to the facts of pathology, which would not fitly be in place here, they are found to furnish the fullest confirmation of what might have

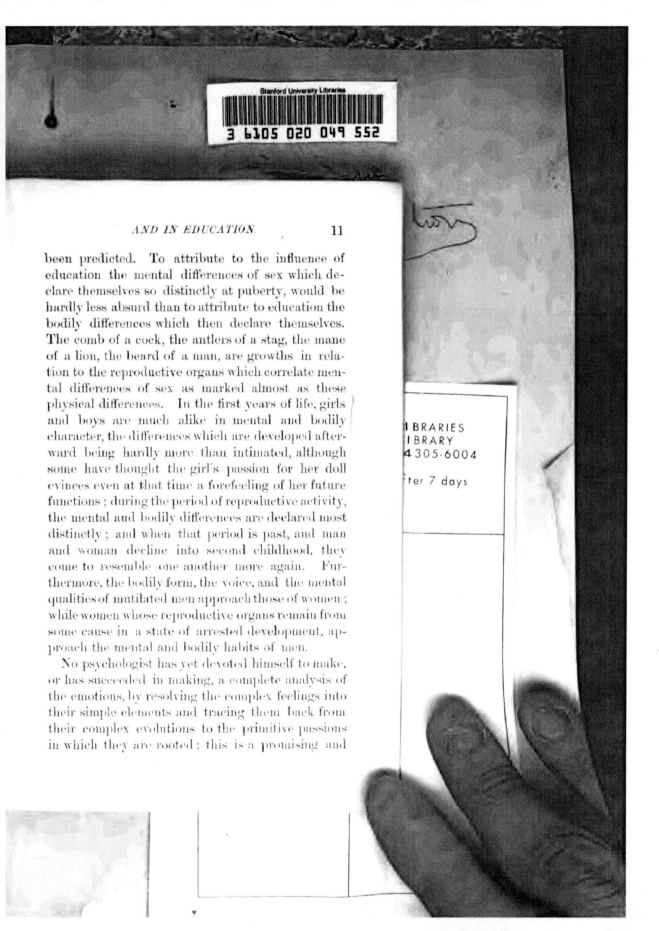

been predicted. To attribute to the influence of
education the mental differences of sex which declare themselves so distinctly at puberty, would be
hardly less absurd than to attribute to education the
bodily differences which then declare themselves.
The comb of a cock, the antlers of a stag, the mane
of a lion, the beard of a man, are growths in relation to the reproductive organs which correlate mental differences of sex as marked almost as these
physical differences. In the first years of life, girls
and boys are much alike in mental and bodily
character, the differences which are developed after-
ward being hardly more than intimated, although
some have thought the girl's passion for her doll
evinces even at that time a forefeeling of her future
functions ; during the period of reproductive activity,
the mental and bodily differences are declared most
distinctly ; and when that period is past, and man
and woman decline into second childhood, they
come to resemble one another more again. Furthermore, the bodily form, the voice, and the mental
qualities of mutilated men approach those of women ;
while women whose reproductive organs remain from
some cause in a state of arrested development, approach the mental and bodily habits of men.

No psychologist has yet devoted himself to make,
or has succeeded in making, a complete analysis of
the emotions, by resolving the complex feelings into
their simple elements and tracing them back from
their complex evolutions to the primitive passions
in which they are rooted ; this is a promising and

much-needed work which remains to be done; but,
when it is done, it will be shown probably that they
have proceeded originally from two fundamental
instincts, or—if we add consciousness of nature
and aim—passions, namely, that of self-preservation, with the ways and means of self-defense which
it inspires and stimulates, and that of propagation,
with the love of offspring and other primitive feeling that are connected with it. Could we in imag-
ination trace mankind backward along the path
stretching through the ages, on which it has gone
forward to its present height and complexity of
emotion, and suppose each new emotional element
to be given off at the spot where it was acquired,
we should view a road along which the fragments of
our high, special, and complex feeling were scattered, and should reach a starting-point of the
primitive instincts of self-preservation and propagation. Considering, then, the different functions
of the sexes in the operation of the latter instinct,
and how a different emotional nature has neces-
sarily been grafted on the original differences in the
course of ages,* does it not appear that in order
to assimilate the female to the male mind it would
be necessary to undo the life-history of mankind
from its earliest commencement? Nay, would it
not be necessary to go still further back to that

---

* The instinct of propagation is what we are concerned with
here, but it should not be overlooked that, in like manner, a
difference of character would grow out of the instinct of self-
preservation and the means of self-defense prompted by it.

earliest period of animal life upon earth before there was any distinction of sex?

If the foregoing reflections be well-grounded, it is plain we ought to recognize sex in education, and to provide that the method and aim of mental culture should have regard to the specialities of woman's physical and mental nature. Each sex must develop after its kind; and if education in its fundamental meaning be the external cause to which evolution is the internal answer, if it be the drawing out of the internal qualities of the individual into their highest perfection by the influence of the most fitting external conditions, there must be a difference in the method of education of the two sexes answering to the differences in their physical and mental natures. Whether it be only the statement of a partial truth, that "for valor he" is formed, and "for beauty she and sweet attractive grace," or not, it cannot be denied that they are formed for different functions, and that the influence of these functions pervades and effects essentially their entire beings. There is sex in mind, and there should be sex in education.

Let us consider, then, what an adapted education must have regard to. In the first place, a proper regard to the physical nature of women means attention given, in their training, to their peculiar functions and to their foreordained work as mothers and nurses of children. Whatever aspirations of an intellectual kind they may have, they cannot be relieved from the performance of those offices so long as it is thought necessary that mankind should continue on earth. Even if these be looked upon as somewhat mean and unworthy offices in comparison with the nobler functions of giving birth to and developing ideas ; if, agreeing with Goethe, we are disposed to hold— " Es wäre doch immer hübscher wenn man die Kinder von den Baumen schüttelte ; " it must still be confessed that for the great majority of women they must remain the most important offices of the best period of their lives. Moreover, they are work which, like all work, may be well or ill done, and which, in order to be done well, cannot be done in a perfunctory manner, as a thing by the way. It will have to be considered whether women can scorn delights, and live laborious days of intellectual exercise and production, without injury to their functions as the conceivers, mothers, and nurses of children. For, it would be an ill thing, if it should so happen that we got the advantages of a quantity of female intellectual work at the price of a puny, enfeebled, and sickly race. In this relation, it must be allowed that women do not and cannot stand on the same level as men.

In the second place, a proper regard to the mental nature of woman means attention given to those qualities of mind which correlate the physical differences of her sex. Men are manifestly not so fitted mentally as women to be the educators of children during the early years of their infancy and childhood ; they would be almost as much out of place in going systematically to work to nurse babies as they would in attempting to suckle them. On the other hand, women are manifestly endowed with qualities of mind which specially fit them to stimulate and foster the first growths of intelligence in children, while the intimate and special sympathies which a mother has with her child as a being which, though individually separate, is still almost a part of her nature, give her an influence and responsibilities which are specially her own. The earliest dawn of an infant's intelligence is its recognition of its mother as the supplyer of its wants, as the person whose near presence is associated with the relief of sensations of discomfort, and with the production of feelings of comfort; while the relief and pleasure which she herself feels in yielding it warmth and nourishment, strengthen, if they were not originally the foundation of, that strong love of offspring which with unwearied patience surrounds its wayward youth with a thousand ministering attentions. It can hardly be doubted that, if the nursing of babies were given over to men for a generation or two, they would abandon the task in despair or in disgust, and conclude it to be not worth while that mankind should continue on earth. But "can a woman forget her sucking child, that she should not have compassion on the son of her womb?" Those can hardly be in earnest who question that woman's sex is represented in mind, and that the mental qualities which spring from it qualify her especially to be the successful nurse and educator of infants and young children.

Furthermore, the female qualities of mind which correlate her sexual character adapt her, as her sex does, to be the helpmate and companion of man. It was an Eastern idea, which Plato has expressed allegorically, that a complete being had in primeval times been divided into two halves, which have ever since been seeking to unite together and to reconstitute the divided unity. It will hardly be denied that there is a great measure of truth in the fable. Man and woman do complement one another's being. This is no less true of mind than it is of body; is true of mind indeed as a consequence of its being true of body. Some may be disposed to argue that the qualities of mind which characterize women now, and have characterized them hitherto, in their relations with men, are in great measure, mainly if not entirely, the artificial results of the position of subjection and dependence which she has always occupied; but those who take this view do not appear to have considered the matter as deeply as they should; they have attributed to circumstances much of what unquestionably lies deeper than circumstances, being inherent in the fundamental character of sex. It would be a delusive hope to expect, and a mistaken labor to attempt, to eradicate by change of circumstances the qualities which distinguish the female character, and fit woman to be the helpmate and companion of man in mental and bodily union.

So much may be fairly said on general physiological grounds. We may now go on to inquire whether any ill effects have been observed from subjecting women to the same kind of training as men. The facts of experience in this country are not such as warrant a full and definite answer to the inquiry, the movement for revolutionizing the education of women being of a recent date. But in America the same method of training for the sexes in mixed classes has been largely applied; girls have gone with boys through the same curriculum of study, from primary to grammar schools, from schools to graduation in colleges, working early under the stimulus of competition, and disdaining any privilege of sex. With what results? With one result certainly—that, while those who are advocates of the mixed system bear favorable witness to the results upon both sexes, American physicians are beginning to raise their voices in earnest warnings and protests. It is not that girls have not ambition, nor that they fail generally to run the intellectual race which is set before them, but it is asserted that they do it at a cost to their strength and health which entails life-long suffering, and even incapacitates them for the adequate performance of the natural functions of their sex. Without pretending to indorse these assertions, which it would be wrong to do in the absence of sufficient experience, it is right to call attention to them, and to claim serious consideration for them; they proceed from physicians of high professional standing, who speak from their own experience, and they agree, moreover, with what perhaps might have been feared or pre-

dicted on physiological grounds. It may fairly be
presumed that the stimulus of competition will act
more powerfully on girls than on boys; not only
because they are more susceptible by nature, but
because it will produce more effect upon their con-
stitutions when it is at all in excess. Their nerve-
centers being in a state of greater instability, by
reason of the development of their reproductive
functions, they will be the more easily and the more
seriously deranged. A great argument used in
favor of a mixed education is that it affords adequate stimulants to girls for thorough and sustained
work, which have hitherto been a want in girls'
schools; that it makes them less desirous to fit
themselves only for society, and content to remain
longer and work harder at school. Thus it is de-
sired that emulation should be used in order to
stimulate them to compete with boys in mental exercises and aims, while it is not pretended they can
or should compete with them in those out-door
exercises and pursuits which are of such great ben-
efit in ministering to bodily health, and to success
in which boys, not unwisely perhaps, attach scarcely
less honor than to intellectual success. It is plain,
then, that the stimulus of competition in studies
will act more powerfully upon them, not only because of their greater constitutional susceptibility,
but because it is left free to act without the com-
pensating balance of emulation in other fields of
activity. Is it right, may well be asked, that it
should be so applied? Can woman rise high in

spiritual development of any kind unless she take a holy care of the temple of her body ? *

A small volume, entitled "Sex in Education," which has been published recently by Dr. Edward Clarke, of Boston, formerly a professor in Harvard College, contains a somewhat startling description of the baneful effects upon female health which have been produced by an excessive educational strain. It is asserted that the number of female graduates of schools and colleges who have been permanently disabled to a greater or less degree by improper methods of study, and by a disregard of the reproductive apparatus and its functions, is so great as to excite the gravest alarm, and to demand the serious attention of the community. "If these causes should continue for the next half-century, and increase in the same ratio as they have for the last fifty years, it requires no prophet to foretell that the wives who are to be the mothers in our republic must be drawn from transatlantic homes. The sons of the New World will have to react, on a magnificent scale, the old story of unwived Rome and the Sabines." Dr. Clarke relates the clinical histories of several cases of tedious illness, in which

---

* Of all the intellectual errors of which men have been guilty, perhaps none is more false and has been more mischievous in its consequences than the theologico-metaphysical doctrine which inculcated contempt of the body as the temple of Satan, the prison-house of the spirit, from which the highest aspiration of mind was to get free. It is a foolish and fruitless labor to attempt to divorce or put asunder mind and body, which Nature has joined together in essential unity ; and the right culture of the body is not less a duty than, is indeed essential to, the right culture of the mind.

he traced the cause unhesitatingly to a disregar
of the function of the female organization. Irreg
ularity, imperfection, arrest, or excess, occurs i
consequence of the demand made upon the vita
powers at times when there should rightly be a
intermission or remission of labor, and is followe
first by pallor, lassitude, debility, sleeplessness
headache, neuralgia, and then by worse ills. The
course of events is something in this wise : The
girl enters upon the hard work of school or college
at the age of fifteen years or thereabouts, when the
function of her sex has perhaps been fairly established ; ambitious to stand high in class, she pur-
sues her studies with diligence, perseverance, con-
stancy, allowing herself no days of relaxation or
rest out of the school-days, paying no attention to
the periodical tides of her organization, unheeding
a drain " that would make the stroke oar of the
university crew falter." For a time all seems to go
well with her studies ; she triumphs over male and
female competitors, gains the front rank, and is
stimulated to continued exertions in order to hold
it. But in the long run Nature, which cannot be
ignored or defied with impunity, asserts its power ;
excessive losses occur ; health fails, she becomes
the victim of aches and pains, is unable to go on
with her work, and compelled to seek medical ad-
vice. Restored to health by rest from work, a holi-
day at the sea-side, and suitable treatment, she
goes back to her studies, to begin again the same
course of unheeding work, until she has completed

the curriculum, and leaves college a good scholar
but a delicate and ailing woman, whose future life
is one of more or less suffering. For she does not
easily regain the vital energy which was recklessly
sacrificed in the acquirement of learning; the special functions which have relation to her future
offices as woman, and the full and perfect accom-
plishment of which is essential to sexual complete-
ness, have been deranged at a critical time; if she
is subsequently married, she is unfit for the best
discharge of maternal functions, and is apt to suffer
from a variety of troublesome and serious disorders
in connection with them. In some cases the brain
and the nervous system testify to the exhaustive
efforts of undue labor, nervous and even mental
disorders declaring themselves.

Such is a picture, painted by an experienced
physician, of the effects of subjecting young women
to the method of education which has been framed
for young men. Startling as it is, there is nothing
in it which may not well be true to Nature. If it
be an effect of excessive and ill-regulated study to
produce derangement of the functions of the female
organization, of which so far from there being an
antecedent improbability there is a great probability,
then there can be no question that all the subse-
quent ills mentioned are likely to follow. The important physiological change which takes place at
puberty, accompanied, as it is, by so great a revolution in mind and body, and by so large an expenditure of vital energy, may easily and quickly over-

3

step its healthy limits and pass into a pathological change, under conditions of excessive stimulation, or in persons who are constitutionally feeble and whose nerve-centers are more unstable than natural ; and it is a familiar medical observation that many nervous disorders of a minor kind, and even such serious disorders as chorea, epilepsy, insanity, are often connected with irregularities or suppression of these important functions.

In addition to the ill effects upon the bodily health which are produced directly by an excessive mental application, and a consequent development of the nervous system at the expense of the nutritive functions, it is alleged that remoter effects of an injurious character are produced upon the entire nature, mental and bodily. The arrest of development of the reproductive system discovers itself in the physical form and in the mental character. There is an imperfect development of the structure which Nature has provided in the female for nursing her offspring.

" Formerly," writes another American physician, Dr. N. Allen, " such an organization was generally possessed by American women, and they found but little difficulty in nursing their infants. It was only occasionally in case of some defect in the organization, or where sickness of some kind had overtaken the mother, that it became necessary to resort to the wet-nurse, or to feeding by hand. And the English, the Scotch, the German, the Canadian, the French, and the Irish women who are living in this country, generally nurse their children ; the exceptions are rare. But how is it with our American women who become mothers ? It has been supposed by some that all, or nearly all of them, could nurse their offspring just as well

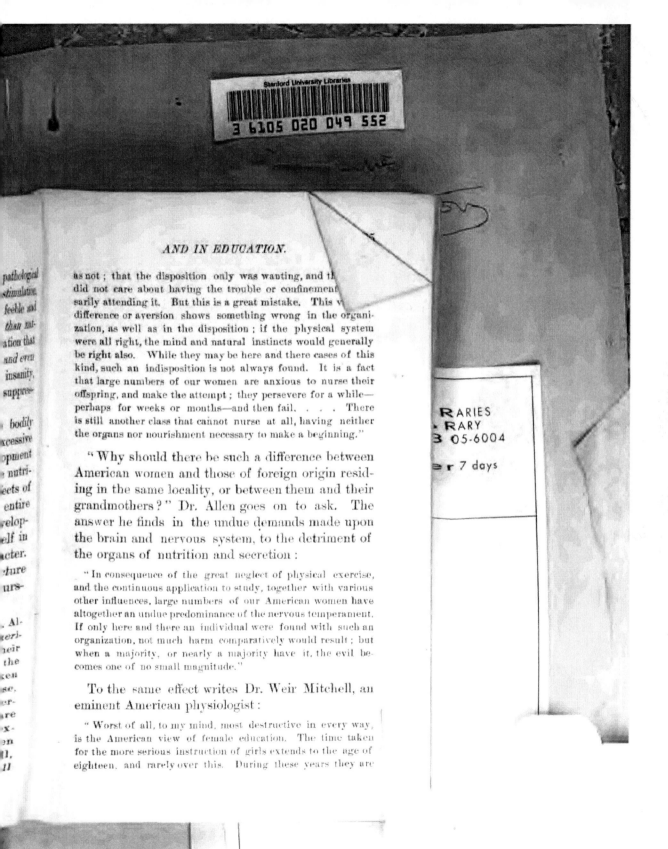

as not ; that the disposition only was wanting, and th[...]
did not care about having the trouble or confinement[...]
sarily attending it. But this is a great mistake. This v[...]
difference or aversion shows something wrong in the organization, as well as in the disposition ; if the physical system
were all right, the mind and natural instincts would generally
be right also. While they may be here and there cases of this
kind, such an indisposition is not always found. It is a fact
that large numbers of our women are anxious to nurse their
offspring, and make the attempt ; they persevere for a while—
perhaps for weeks or months—and then fail. . . . There
is still another class that cannot nurse at all, having neither
the organs nor nourishment necessary to make a beginning."

"Why should there be such a difference between
American women and those of foreign origin resid-
ing in the same locality, or between them and their
grandmothers?" Dr. Allen goes on to ask. The
answer he finds in the undue demands made upon
the brain and nervous system, to the detriment of
the organs of nutrition and secretion :

"In consequence of the great neglect of physical exercise,
and the continuous application to study, together with various
other influences, large numbers of our American women have
altogether an undue predominance of the nervous temperament.
If only here and there an individual were found with such an
organization, not much harm comparatively would result ; but
when a majority, or nearly a majority have it, the evil becomes one of no small magnitude."

To the same effect writes Dr. Weir Mitchell, an
eminent American physiologist :

"Worst of all, to my mind, most destructive in every way,
is the American view of female education. The time taken
for the more serious instruction of girls extends to the age of
eighteen, and rarely over this. During these years they are

undergoing such organic development as renders them remarkably sensitive. . . . To-day the American woman is, to speak plainly, physically unfit for her duties as woman, and is, perhaps, of all civilized females, the least qualified to undertake those weightier tasks which tax so heavily the nervous system of man. She is not fairly up to what Nature asks from her as a wife and mother. How will she sustain herself under the pressure of those yet more exacting duties which nowadays she is eager to share with man?"

Here, then, is no uncertain testimony as to the effects of the American system of female education: some women who are without the instinct or desire to nurse their offspring, some who have the desire but not the capacity, and others who have neither the instinct nor the capacity. The facts will hardly be disputed, whatever may finally be the accepted interpretation of them. It will not probably be argued that an absence of the capacity and the instinct to nurse is a result of higher development, and that it should be the aim of woman, as she advances to a higher level, to allow the organs which minister to this function to waste and finally to become by disuse as rudimentary in her sex as they are in the male sex. Their development is notably in close sympathy with that of the organs of reproduction, an arrest thereof being often associated with some defect of the latter; so that it might perhaps fairly be questioned whether it was right and proper, for the race's sake, that a woman who has not the wish or power to nurse should indulge in the functions of maternity. We may take note, by-the-way, that those in whom the organs are wasted invoke the dressmaker's aid in order to gain the appearance of them; they are not satisfied unless they wear the show of perfect womanhood. However, it may be in the plan of evolution to produce at some future period a race of sexless beings who, undistracted and unharassed by the ignoble troubles of reproduction, shall carry on the intellectual work of the world, not otherwise than as the sexless ants do the work and the fighting of the community.

Meanwhile, the consequences of an imperfectly developed reproductive system are not sexual only; they are also mental. Intellectually and morally there is a deficiency, or at any rate a modification answering to the physical deficiency; in mind, as in body, the individual fails to reach the ideal of a complete and perfect womanhood. If the aim of a true education be to make her reach *that*, it cannot certainly be a true education which operates in any degree to unsex her; for sex is fundamental, lies deeper than culture, cannot be ignored or defied with impunity. You may hide Nature, but you cannot extinguish it. Consequently, it does not seem impossible that, if the attempt to do so be seriously and persistently made, the result may be a monstrosity—something which having ceased to be woman is yet not man—" ce quelque chose de monstrueux," which the Comte A. de Gasparin forebodes, " cet être répugnant, qui déjà paraît à notre horizon."

The foregoing considerations go to show that the

main reason of woman's position lies in her nature. That she has not competed with men in the active work of life was probably because, not having had the power, she had not the desire to do so, and because, having the capacity of functions which man has not, she has found her pleasure in performing them. It is not simply that man, being stronger in body than she is, has held her in subjection, and debarred her from careers of action which he was resolved to keep for himself; her maternal functions must always have rendered, and must continue to render, most of her activity domestic. There have been times enough in the history of the world, when the freedom which she has had, and the position which she has held in the estimation of men, would have enabled her to assert her claims to other functions, had she so willed it. The most earnest advocate of her rights to be something else than what she has hitherto been would hardly argue that she has always been in the position of a slave kept in forcible subjection by the superior physical force of men. Assuredly, if she has been a slave she has been a slave content with her bondage. But it may perhaps be said that in that lies the very pith of the matter—that she is not free, and does not care to be free; that she is a slave, and does not know or feel it. It may be alleged that she has lived for so many ages in the position of dependence to which she was originally reduced by the superior muscular strength of man, has been so thoroughly imbued with inherit-

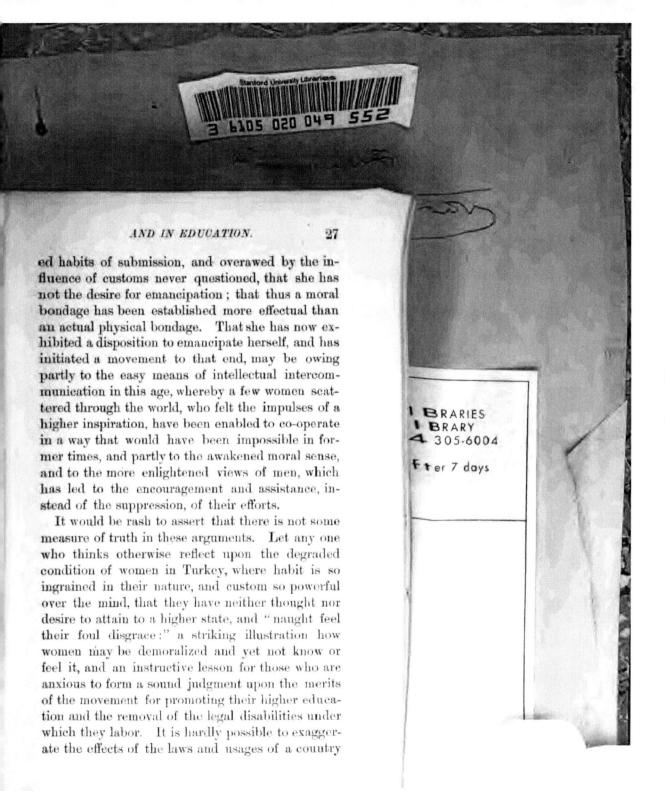

ed habits of submission, and overawed by the influence of customs never questioned, that she has not the desire for emancipation ; that thus a moral bondage has been established more effectual than an actual physical bondage. That she has now exhibited a disposition to emancipate herself, and has initiated a movement to that end, may be owing partly to the easy means of intellectual intercommunication in this age, whereby a few women scattered through the world, who felt the impulses of a higher inspiration, have been enabled to co-operate in a way that would have been impossible in former times, and partly to the awakened moral sense, and to the more enlightened views of men, which has led to the encouragement and assistance, instead of the suppression, of their efforts.

It would be rash to assert that there is not some measure of truth in these arguments. Let any one who thinks otherwise reflect upon the degraded condition of women in Turkey, where habit is so ingrained in their nature, and custom so powerful over the mind, that they have neither thought nor desire to attain to a higher state, and " naught feel their foul disgrace :" a striking illustration how women may be demoralized and yet not know or feel it, and an instructive lesson for those who are anxious to form a sound judgment upon the merits of the movement for promoting their higher education and the removal of the legal disabilities under which they labor. It is hardly possible to exaggerate the effects of the laws and usages of a country upon the habits of thought of those who, generation after generation, have been born, and bred, and have lived under them. Were the law, which ordains that, when a father dies intestate, all the real property of which he is possessed shall be inherited by his eldest son, his other children being sent empty away, enacted for the first time, there is no one, probably, who would not be shocked by its singular injustice; yet the majority of persons in this country are far from thinking it extraordinary or unjust, and a great many of them would deem it a dangerous and wicked doctrine to question its justice. Only a few weeks ago, a statesman who has held high offices in a Conservative ministry, in an address to electors, conjured them not to part with the principle of primogeniture, and declared that there was no change in the law which he would so vehemently oppose as this: "Let them but follow the example of a neighboring nation in this respect, and there was an end of their personal freedom and liberty!" So much do the laws and usages of a country affect the feelings and judgments of those who dwell therein. If we clearly apprehend the fact, and allow it the weight which it deserves, it will be apparent that we must hesitate to accept the subordinate position which women have always had as a valid argument for the justice of it, and a sufficient reason why they should continue forever in it.

But may we not fairly assert that it would be no less a mistake in an opposite direction to allow no

weight to such an argument? Setting physiological considerations aside, it is not possible to suppose that the whole explanation of woman's position
and character is that man, having in the beginning
found her pleasing in his eyes and necessary to his
enjoyment, took forcible possession of her, and has
ever since kept her in bondage, without any other
justification than the right of the strongest. Superiority of muscular strength, without superiority
of any other kind, would not have done that, any
more than superiority of muscular strength has
availed to give the lion or the elephant possession
of the earth. If it were not that woman's organization and functions found their fitting home in a position different from, if not subordinate to, that of
men, she would not so long have kept that position.
If she is to be judged by the same standard as men,
and to make their aims her aims, we are certainly
bound to say that she labors under an inferiority of
constitution by a dispensation which there is no gain-
saying. This is a matter of physiology, not a matter
of sentiment; it is not a mere question of larger or
smaller muscles, but of the energy and power of
endurance of the nerve-force which drives the intellectual and muscular machinery; not a question of
two bodies and minds that are in equal physical
conditions, but of one body and mind capable of
sustained and regular hard labor, and of another
body and mind which for one quarter of each month
during the best years of life is more or less sick and
unfit for hard work. It is in these considerations

that we find the true explanation of what has been
from the beginning until now, and what must doubt-
less continue to be, though it be in a modified form.
It may be a pity for woman that she has been
created woman, but, being such, it is as ridiculous
to consider herself inferior to man because she is
not man, as it would be for man to consider himself
inferior to her because he cannot perform her functions. There is one glory of the man, another glory
of the woman, and the glory of the one differeth
from that of the other.

Taking into adequate account the physiology of
the female organization, some of the statements
made by the late Mr. Mill in his book on the subjection of women strike one with positive amaze-
ment. He calls upon us to own that what is now
called the nature of women is an eminently artificial
thing, the result of forced repression in some direc-
tions, of unnatural stimulation in others; that their
character has been entirely distorted and disguised
by their relations with their masters, who have kept
them in so unnatural a state; that if it were not for
this there would not be any material difference, nor
perhaps any difference at all, in the character and
capacities which would unfold themselves; that
they would do the same things as men fully as well
on the whole, if education and cultivation were
adapted to correcting, instead of aggravating, the
infirmities incident to their temperament; and that
they have been robbed of their natural development, and brought into their present unnatural

state, by the brutal right of the strongest, which man has used. If these allegations contain no exaggeration, if they be strictly true, then is this article an entire mistake.

Mr. Mill argues as if, when he has shown it to be probable that the inequality of rights between the sexes has no other source than the law of the strongest, he had demonstrated its monstrous injustice. But is that entirely so? After all, there is a right in might—the right of the strong to be strong. Men have the right to make the most of their powers, to develop them to the utmost, and to strive for, and if possible gain and hold, the position in which they shall have the freest play. It would be a wrong to the stronger if it were required to limit its exertions to the capacities of the weaker. And if it be not so limited, the result will be that the weaker must take a different position. Men will not fail to take the advantage of their strength over women : are no laws, then, to be made which, owning the inferiority of women's strength, shall ordain accordingly, and so protect them really from the mere brutal tyranny of might? Seeing that the greater power cannot be ignored, but in the long-run must tell in individual competition, it is a fair question whether it ought not to be recognized in social adjustments and enactments, even for the necessary protection of women. Suppose that all legal distinctions were abolished, and that women were allowed free play to do what they could, as it may be right they should—to fail or succeed in every career upon which men enter; that all were conceded to them which their extremest advocates might claim for them; do they imagine that, if they, being in a majority, combined to pass laws which were unwelcome to men, the latter would quietly submit? Is it proposed that men should fight for them in war, and that they, counting a majority of votes, should determine upon war? Or would they no longer claim a privilege of sex in regard to the defence of the country by arms? If all barriers of distinction of sex raised by human agency were thrown down, as not being warranted by the distinctions of sex which Nature has so plainly marked, it may be presumed that the great majority of women would continue to discharge the functions of maternity, and to have the mental qualities which correlate these functions; and if laws were made by them, and their male supporters of a feminine habit of mind, in the interest of babies, as might happen, can it be supposed that, as the world goes, there would not soon be a revolution in the state by men, which would end in taking all power from women and reducing them to a stern subjection? Legislation would not be of much value unless there were power behind to make it respected, and in such case laws might be made without the power to enforce them, or for the very purpose of coercing the power which could alone enforce them.

So long as the differences of physical power and organization between men and women are what they are, it does not seem possible that they should have

the same type of mental development. But while
we see great reason to dissent from the opinions,
and to distrust the enthusiasm, of those who would
set before women the same aims as men, to be pur-
sued by the same methods, it must be admitted that
they are entitled to have all the mental culture and
all the freedom necessary to the fullest development of their natures. The aim of female education should manifestly be the perfect development,
not of manhood but of womanhood, by the methods most conducive thereto: so may women reach
as high a grade of development as men, though it
be of a different type. A system of education
which is framed to fit them to be nothing more than
the superintendents of a household and the orna-
ments of a drawing-room, is one which does not do
justice to their nature, and cannot be seriously de-
fended. Assuredly those of them who have not the
opportunity of getting married suffer not a little, in
mind and body, from a method of education which
tends to develop the emotional at the expense of
the intellectual nature, and by their exclusion from
appropriate fields of practical activity. It by no
means follows, however, that it would be right to
model an improved system exactly upon that which
has commended itself as the best for men. Inas-
much as the majority of women will continue to
get married and to discharge the functions of mothers, the education of girls certainly ought not to be
such as would in any way clash with their organization, injure their health, and unfit them for these

functions. In this matter the small minority of women who have other aims and pant for other careers, cannot be accepted as the spokeswomen of their sex. Experience may be left to teach them, as it will not fail to do, whether they are right or wrong in the ends which they pursue and in the means by which they pursue them : if they are right, they will have deserved well the success which will reward their faith and works ; if they are wrong, the error will avenge itself upon them and upon their children, if they should ever have any. In the worst event they will not have been without their use as failures ; for they will have furnished experiments to aid us in arriving at correct judgments concerning the capacities of women and their right functions in the universe. Meanwhile, so far as our present lights reach, it would seem that a system of education adapted to women should have regard to the peculiarities of their constitution, to the special functions in life for which they are destined, and to the range and kind of practical activity, mental and bodily, to which they would seem to be foreordained by their sexual organization of body and mind.

NOTE.—It is fair to say that other reasons for the alleged degeneracy of American women are given. For example, a correspondent writes from America : " The medical mind of the United States is arrayed in a very ill-tempered opposition, on assumed physiological grounds, to the higher education of women in a continuous curriculum, and especially to that coeducation which some colleges in the Western States, Oberlin, Antioch, inaugurated twenty years ago, and which latterly Cornell University has adopted. The experience of Cornell is too recent to prove any thing; but the Quaker college of Swarthmore claims a steady improvement on the health of its girl-graduates, dating from the commencement of their college course; and the Western colleges report successful results, mentally, morally, and physically, from their coeducation experiment. Ignoring these facts, the doctors base their war-cry on the not-to-be-disputed fact that American women are growing into more and more of invalidism with every year. Something of this is perhaps due to climate. I will not say to food; for the American *menu*, in the cities at least, has improved since Mr. Dickens's early days, and has learned to combine French daintiness, very happily, with the substantial requirements of an English table.

"American men, as a rule, 'break down' between forty and fifty, when an Englishman is but beginning to live his public and useful life. The mad excitement of business you have, as well as we; so it must be the unrest of the climate, and their unphilosophical refusal of open air pleasures and exercise, which are to blame in the case of the men.

"There are other reasons which go to make up the languid young-ladyhood of the American girl.

Her childhood is denied the happy out-door sports of her brothers. There is a resolute shutting out of everything like a noisy romp; the active games and all happy, boisterous plays, by field or road-side, are not *proper* to her! She is cased in a cramp-ing dress, so heavy and inconvenient that no boy could wear it for a day without falling into gloomy views of life. All this martyrdom to propriety. and fashion tells upon strength and symmetry, and the girl reaches womanhood a wreck. That she reaches it at all, under these suffering and bleached-out conditions, is due to her superior elasticity to resist a method of education which would have killed off all the boys years before. . . . There are abundant statistics to prove that hard study is the discipline and tonic most girls need to supplant the too great sentimentality and useless day-dreams fostered by fashionable idleness, and provocative of ' nerves,' melancholy, and inanition generally, and, so far as statistics can, that the women-gradu-ates of these colleges make as healthy and happy wives and mothers as though they had never solved a mathematical problem, nor translated Aristotle."
—*Fortnightly Review.*

CPSIA information can be obtained at www.ICGtesting.com
Printed in the USA
BVOW04s1134200416

444940BV00018B/336/P